Time Management

Ongoing Enhancement Of Time Management Strategies, Facilitating The Attainment Of Optimal Efficiency

(Efficient Techniques For Enhancing Productivity, Overcoming Procrastination)

Vinzenz Tanzer

TABLE OF CONTENT

The Phenomenon Of Persistent Postponement 1

Strategies And Techniques For Enhancing Group Efficiency Through Time Management Activities And Exercises 18

Esteemed Methodologies In The Corporate World For Enhancing Employee Motivation 31

Time Saving Habits 48

Crucial Time Management Skills To Achieve Workplace Success 81

Nothing Happens Overnight 85

Leveraging Your Task List For Establishing Goals And Deadlines 98

Overcoming Procrastination 104

However, The Vast Majority Of Individuals Tend To Engage In Procrastination. Why? 119

Divide Larger Projects Into Smaller Components 142

The Physical Aspect Of Time Management 146

Options For Work-Life Balance 152

The Phenomenon Of Persistent Postponement

Lately, I have devoted considerable contemplation to the subject of procrastination, exploring both its underlying causes and potential remedies.

What are the factors contributing to the phenomenon of procrastination? Through my investigation, I have identified several factors that contribute significantly to procrastination. However, two factors in particular stand out as major contributors: perfectionism and impulsivity.

The concepts underlying these two potential causes are quite evident.

Procrastination can occur as a result of perfectionism, as individuals with perfectionistic tendencies may struggle to initiate or complete tasks due to the belief that the outcome will never meet their exceedingly high and impractical standards. Makes sense?

In individuals prone to impulsivity, procrastination stems from their incapacity to diligently apply themselves and concentrate on one task at a time. It corresponds to the theory of procrastination often referred to as the 'distracting allure of shiny objects'. The impulsive procrastinator may often engage in concurrent pursuits or hastily initiate new endeavors as a means of evading the potentially less gratifying tasks.

To what extent do the concepts of "perfectionism" and "impulsivity" serve as plausible explanations for the occurrence of procrastination?

Let's start with perfectionism. Does perfectionism cause procrastination? Certainly it does... to varying degrees. It exerts a greater influence on certain individuals compared to others. Undoubtedly, this issue arises from the theory's inherent flaw: Not all individuals exhibit perfectionistic tendencies. Individuals of all backgrounds are prone to procrastination to varying extents.

This implies that perfectionism does not encompass the entirety of the narrative.

What if we consider impulsivity as the underlying factor leading to procrastination? This assertion is equally valid, although I believe it fails to account for the entirety of the phenomenon of procrastination. Take into account the existence of prolonged procrastination that spans months or even years - this phenomenon cannot be simply ascribed to impulsivity. This type of procrastination necessitates genuine commitment. Ironically, diligent effort is required in this endeavor.

No, impulsivity is also an integral aspect of the narrative regarding procrastination.

The Essence of Procrastination

The further my analysis extends, the more evident it becomes that the phenomenon of procrastination bears significant parallels to cancer. Just as there exist numerous types and variations of procrastination, they all fall within the overarching classification of "procrastination."

The potential cause of procrastination is unlikely to be attributed to any specific psychological trait, such as perfectionism or impulsivity. It would be desirable to identify a singular causative factor; however, it is not as straightforward as it may seem.

No, procrastination is not merely caused by external factors, it is inherent to our nature and existence. It is an intrinsic characteristic of the human race.

Certainly, I believe the core essence of procrastination can be attributed to our fundamental evolution as a species. This phenomenon could potentially elucidate why procrastination permeates the lives of individuals universally.

One must understand that humans are inherently not predisposed to engaging in extensive, forward-thinking endeavors. The habitat in which our nomadic predecessors resided did not present numerous incentives to formulate long-term plans extending beyond a few weeks to a few months ahead. Their strategies typically revolved around immediate or near-immediate gratification as the reward, often driven by short-term objectives or reactive measures to perceived threats.

While this lends some credibility to the theory associating procrastination with impulsivity, it is evident that individuals possess the capacity to implement long-term strategies. It is simply not a strength that we possess as a species.

My assertion is that allocating time to identify "causes" of procrastination is not a productive use of time. There exists an inexhaustible plethora of justifications for the act of procrastination.

It would be advisable, in my opinion, to ascertain whether you fall within one of two distinct categories of procrastination pertaining to a particular subject.

The Contrast between Basic Procrastination and Chronic Procrastination

There exists a discernible contrast between two distinct categories of procrastination: simple and chronic.

Primary procrastination is characterized by a mere lack of motivation to engage in a task due to its tedious, inconvenient, or unpleasant nature. It can be suitably explicated by deficient impulse regulation, perfectionism, or an inability to engage in long-term strategizing, for instance.

Various methods can be employed to overcome ordinary procrastination, a few of which will be delineated in the subsequent discussion.

Let us consider the concept of persistent procrastination - such as continually delaying the task of filing taxes for several years, or the inability to successfully complete a relatively straightforward home improvement project over the course of an entire summer.

This form of procrastination gradually consumes several months or even years of valuable time and has the potential to greatly disrupt individuals' lives. It is widespread and is a significant cause of stress. It exhibits a high level of resistance against most endeavors to surmount it.

In my opinion, the fundamental cause of chronic procrastination lies in experiencing a sense of being "disrupted" or a form of underlying apprehension. This sensation manifests itself regardless of one's conscious acknowledgement or understanding, and regardless of its logical coherence as a subjective experience.

Put simply, when individuals consistently put off tasks, such as unpaid taxes or unfinished projects, they perceive them as significant risks, which activates a profound instinctual motivation to evade them.

Chronic procrastination may stem from a perceived existential threat. That is to say, the mind has unequivocally linked the act of engaging in that particular action, regardless of its nature, with the possibility of mortal consequences.

Curing Procrastination

If my previous speculation is accurate, it appears that our only course of action is to work towards mitigating procrastination. If procrastination indeed arises from an inherent genetic predisposition within our species, there exists no viable "remedy," aside from the potential passage of a few million years of further evolution. Maybe not even then.

One approach that many individuals resort to for mitigation is technological solutions such as productivity applications and other strategies. This proves to be an effective solution, as several of these systems are indeed valuable in aiding individuals. If it proves efficacious for you, then it is efficacious for you. However, it can effectively assist in addressing only temporary procrastination. Chronic procrastination poses a significant challenge for productivity-enhancing strategies.

One alternative is to utilize negative reinforcement (disciplinary actions). This represents the method of forcefully addressing procrastination, and it does yield results for a certain duration. A demonstration of employing adverse motivation upon oneself could involve formulating a plan to contribute funds to a political party that one strongly dislikes, in the event of failing to accomplish a specific objective. Disagreeable and verging on self-harm, albeit with potential efficacy.

What about positive motivation?

Initially, if one were already inclined towards a positive mindset, the phenomenon of procrastination would cease to be a concern. Therefore, is there a means to "generate" positive motivation, so to speak? Is it plausible to develop a positive inclination towards pursuing a task, notwithstanding an initial lack of enthusiasm?

Yes, there is. After initiating a task, it becomes more manageable to sustain the momentum, as an illustration. Indeed, it is increasingly gratifying to persevere in the completion of a task or project, even if it does not pertain to a field of personal interest or preference. Individuals are innately predisposed to exhibit a greater propensity for continued engagement with a project once initiated, as evidenced by a research conducted by Kenneth McGraw.

Certainly, initiating a task or project can in itself pose a challenge--a topic that I believe warrants further exploration in the future.

Several of the aforementioned alternatives are effective, with some demonstrating notable efficacy, for the purpose of addressing minor instances of postponement. The issue of chronic procrastination presents a significant challenge to address, given its pervasive and all-encompassing nature.

For instance, it is not viable to employ significant negative incentives when dealing with an individual who engages in tax avoidance, as they are already subjected to severe penalties, including substantial fines and potential imprisonment. Therefore, it becomes imperative to question the effectiveness of further negative motivation in such cases. However, they continue to delay their tasks despite the prospect of these possible consequences. Purchasing a productivity application for their iPhone would yield questionable advantages, to express it diplomatically.

Positive motivation does not play a significant role either when the individual who procrastinates consistently opposes any attempts to even address the matter.

How to Achieve Forward Motion in Overcoming Procrastination

All is not hopeless. I believe that both instances of casual procrastination and persistent procrastination can be addressed through the enhancement of attention control and metacognitive abilities.

By increasing your awareness and ability to concentrate on the factors that tend to induce your procrastination, even those of which you may not currently be consciously cognizant, you enhance your prospects, at the very minimum. In the most favorable scenario, you may be able to surmount the challenges that you previously deemed insurmountable.

There are multiple methodologies available to cultivate and refine one's powers of focus. The Pomodoro Technique is an effective method for enhancing attentiveness and cultivating productive work practices.

Although I acknowledge the potential vulnerability of succumbing to a fixation on a single approach, engaging in meditation provides an excellent opportunity to cultivate both focused concentration and enhance metacognitive abilities. It hones your ability to recognize the internal dialogue that serves as a source of distraction, murmurs threatening thoughts, and relentlessly pursues immediate gratification. It enables individuals to recognize that they are not obliged to adhere to those directives, irrespective of their persuasiveness or attractiveness.

Meditation contributes to enhancing emotional attunement, promoting self-awareness of patterns and circumstances that may engender emotional responses.

Through the practice of meditation, I have observed a diminishing attachment to particular thoughts and emotions, regardless of their compelling nature. I find it more manageable to dedicate extended periods of time, spanning weeks or even months, to the pursuit of a specific goal, despite any discomfort or unpleasantness that may accompany it.

Additionally, it is worth noting that the practice of meditation has proven to be instrumental in tackling persistent procrastination in certain areas, offering a profound sense of relief.

Strategies And Techniques For Enhancing Group Efficiency Through Time Management Activities And Exercises

Time management exercises can be advantageous in instructing a collective (and even the individual) on the principles of effective time management and enhanced productivity.

In the forthcoming chapter, we will explore seventeen time management practices that can be employed by individuals and teams to effectively enhance productivity levels.

The Mayo Jar

The mayo jar demonstration exemplifies the significance of prioritizing crucial tasks foremost.

You possess an unoccupied container along with substantial stones, lesser stones, tiny pebbles, fine granules, and liquid.

The subsequent amount of the remaining items you can add is contingent upon the precedence of the objects that are initially placed. By prioritizing the placement of larger tasks, analogous to significant rocks, followed by subsequent items in descending order, one can accommodate a variety of elements within the given space, unlike the scenario where sand is introduced initially, limiting the inclusion of other objects, barring a few instances where water can be encompassed.

Delegation Skill Practice

In the context of this time management exercise, the premise entails the presence of a newly appointed assistant, affording you the opportunity to assign certain tasks to said assistant.

The members are categorized into triads comprising a leader, a worker, and an onlooker. The delegatee engages in the act of delegation, while the onlooker possesses a document designed to provide constructive feedback on the delegatee's performance and offer recommendations for enhancing their delegation abilities. Every individual is given an opportunity.

Dealing with Distractions

Interruptions can have a detrimental impact on one's level of efficiency.

In this exercise, one must ascertain the sources of distractions and subsequently devise strategies to effectively mitigate them.

An alternative approach is to monitor and record the passage of time across several consecutive days. Certainly, it is plausible that you may possess the ability to readily discern certain elements of diversion within your daily existence.

Write them down. Next, dedicate effort towards devising effective approaches to surmount these challenges.

If collective participation is employed, endeavor to collaborate as a unified cohort, either as an entire class or in smaller collective units. Please document the sources of your distractions and subsequently engage in deliberation to identify potential solutions.

Time Squared

Each individual shall receive a total of three pages, each containing 24 squares that meticulously depict the chronological course of the 24 hours.

Participants are required to complete the initial page by documenting their daily routine activities.

The subsequent page pertains to the unproductive time utilized by the employees during working hours.

On the third day, they incorporate the entire contents of the previous two elements onto it. The vacant temporal void is a period of productivity.

They are subsequently able to observe and assess areas where they can decrease or entirely remove tasks, thereby augmenting their overall productive time.

Arrange the Cards

In this particular endeavor, the group shall be partitioned into distinct teams.

Every team will receive a deck of cards and must meticulously arrange them in a predetermined sequence as swiftly as possible, establishing a competitive atmosphere among the teams. They will be allocated a 5-minute timeframe to devise strategic plans, engage in practice sessions, and subsequently participate in three successive rounds.

This exercise imparts the significance of careful planning, the formulation of an effective strategy, and the proficient distribution of tasks.

Circadian Rhythms

In this time allocation exercise, individual participants are provided with a sheet of paper divided into hourly segments. During that period, they subsequently enumerate the various energy states that they are in.

For instance, can they be described as exhibiting a state of heightened activity, reaching a level of accomplishment nearing 70%, experiencing a decline in momentum, and so forth. The objective is to assist individuals in recognizing their periods of peak performance and decline, thereby enabling them to optimize their time more effectively.

Time Wasters

The objective of this endeavor is to acquire the skill of effectively surmounting time-consuming obstacles.

The group is divided into four teams. Every team will receive an envelope containing four index cards, with a time-consuming activity specified on the reverse side of the envelope.

The team is allotted a duration of three minutes to generate as many strategies for mitigating the time-wasting factor and record them on a single index card. Subsequently, the envelope is transferred to the subsequent group, and so forth.

Subsequently, each team may proceed with the presentation of their findings, followed by a collective assessment through a voting process to determine the most exemplary ones, or any other method deemed appropriate to review the results.

Lists & Priorities

In this endeavor, you are presented with a compilation of assignments, each carrying a distinctive points allocation.

The group shall be divided into teams, with each team being given a time limit of 10 minutes to complete the assigned tasks. Subsequently, you calculate the scores. Afterwards, engage in a discussion with them regarding their prioritization methods and related matters.

Puzzle Challenge

You are responsible for arranging your group into smaller teams and assigning them a puzzle task to collaborate on.

Nonetheless, you fail to provide them with a comprehensive portrayal of the image, the overarching perspective. After a brief period of time elapses, you inquire about the deficiencies and obstacles present in the situation. It is probable that they will assert that they lack the visual representation of the intended appearance. Thereafter, you deliver it to them.

The objective of this exercise is to demonstrate the significance of comprehending the overall perspective when strategizing and selecting our undertakings.

Overcoming Undesirable Patterns

In this task, participants collaborate in pairs. Every individual is requested to jot down on a sheet of paper the factors that hinder their ability to manage time more efficiently.

Subsequently, the pair collaborates closely to devise resolutions. Subsequently, you may present it consecutively to the entire assembly.

What is the duration..

There exist multiple approaches to undertake this time management exercise. The objective is to demonstrate how, despite the equitable allocation of time, individuals can perceive and encounter time in disparate manners.

Each individual is required to rise, settle in a seated position, or lift their eyelids once they believe a elapsed duration of one minute has transpired. They will observe that a majority of individuals assume various positions, including sitting, standing, or opening their eyes, at different intervals.

The epitome of excellence: " Ace of Spaces

In the context of this particular activity, two individuals of voluntary nature shall be required along with a duo of card decks.

The two volunteers engage in a competitive pursuit to be the first to locate the Ace of Spaces. The first deck is arranged in a sequential and suit-oriented manner, while the second deck exhibits a jumbled state with certain cards facing the opposite direction, etc.

The objective is to demonstrate the correlation between organization and its impact on both time management and productivity.

The Band

The purpose of this time management exercise is to illustrate the extent of available time in our lives to effectively accomplish tasks.

The ribbon's length symbolizes the duration of our existence. During the course of the activity, portions are deducted for days designated as rest days, sleeping hours, meal times, sick leave, and other such occurrences.

Ultimately, the ribbon appears to be considerably shorter than our initial estimation. It demonstrates the significance of effectively utilizing the time at our disposal.

Monetary worth

Individuals divide their activities into categories of cost and profit centers. Subsequently, they direct their attention towards allocating their time to the endeavors that generate the highest level of worth.

Yesterday's Performance Evaluation Report

Each individual shall record a list comprising of ten activities they have accomplished on the previous day. Subsequently, they proceed to transcribe five subjects that they anticipate delving into during their impending performance evaluation, on a separate sheet of paper. Subsequently, they proceed to review both documents in order to ascertain whether their assigned responsibilities align with the criteria deemed crucial for the purpose of their performance evaluation.

A total of $86,400, or an equivalent sum in any other form of currency, is required.

There exists a plethora of methods to engage in this time management exercise.

Individuals will be provided with an allocation of $86,400 each for their personal expenditures. Alternatively, the option exists for the allocation to be collectively utilized by the team through the means of a flipchart or paper, allowing for collaborative decision-making on how the funds will be expended.

The sole limitation is that it must be expended in its entirety within a single day, otherwise it will be forfeited. You can't save it.

This represents our time. A day consists of a total of 86,400 seconds. When we fail to make prudent investments, we incur losses. It is not possible to reserve time for future use.

Blocks of varying hues

Through this particular task, individuals or groups are required to collect as many blocks as possible within a span of one minute using their non-dominant hand. They are awarded one point for each.

Subsequently, you proceed to replay the game utilizing varied point allocations for distinct hues.

The purpose of this exercise is to impart the skill of prioritization.

Esteemed Methodologies In The Corporate World For Enhancing Employee Motivation

Furthermore, apart from employing applications and adapting our behaviors and approaches, there exist a multitude of corporate methodologies that prove highly effective in enhancing motivation.

Many larger corporations employ incentives to drive employee motivation and encourage success. Regardless of whether you are not the proprietor of a substantial enterprise, you are still capable of implementing incentives in your personal life. Motivate yourself towards success through the establishment of incentives to acknowledge the accomplishment of specific milestones. These incentives may encompass uncomplicated opportunities such as availing a personal day off to unwind or acquiring a fresh purchase of nail polish, yet it is important to select something that genuinely inspires you to persevere in your pursuit of accomplishment.

Recognize Achievements

An additional approach frequently employed by corporations to encourage ongoing dedication and effort from employees is the implementation of recognition as a form of incentive. When an individual receives acknowledgment for their accomplishments, they experience a heightened sense of fulfillment and perceive themselves as being more esteemed for the contributions they have made. Even if you operate as a sole proprietor, you have the ability to instill acknowledgement of accomplishments through the act of disseminating your achievements to loved ones and acquaintances.

Expositions, Conferences, and Continued Professional Development

Trade fairs, conferences, and advanced educational programs are commonly employed strategies to enhance motivation. These events collectively facilitate the establishment of connections among individuals who share similar objectives, while concurrently fostering a sense of higher learning in a specific field of interest. Frequently, these occurrences unveil novel approaches to accomplishing tasks or new breakthroughs that aid in the enhancement of task efficiency. Such discoveries and advancements can act as compelling incentives for many individuals, as they witness the remarkable progress that can be accomplished through their determination and perseverance.

~ ADDRESSED WITHIN THE CONTEXT OF HANDLING INTERFERENCES ~

This aligns perfectly with maintaining a sense of concentration. I have previously addressed the deleterious effects posed by social media, email, and online information; however, there exist additional sources of diversion that warrant discussion. Consider the surrounding environment when diligently applying yourself to achieve a given task. Does that environment offer the most optimal conditions for you to achieve maximum productivity? Maybe you find yourself situated at a disorganized workstation or working remotely, with your children constantly moving about and frequently seeking your undivided focus.

Distractions impede our progress and hinder us from reaching our full potential. Each moment we divert our focus from the current task, we decrease the amount of time available for personal development. The solitary resource that remains consistent for all individuals is time. I am not referring to the duration of an individual's lifespan, however it remains a reality that each person is allotted a fixed span of 24 hours within a day to maximize their accomplishments. Certain individuals opt to allocate 10 hours of their time for sleep, dedicate 2 hours to engaging with social media platforms, meticulously execute every task they undertake, and aimlessly muse about their day without purpose.

You should take it upon yourself to introspect and determine if there exists a more ideal opportunity for pursuing your objectives. I struggle to effectively work remotely in the presence of my other family members at home. Therefore, I have identified multiple coffee establishments in my vicinity that provide me with a more conducive ambience for productivity. In future instances, it would be beneficial to inquire to oneself, "Might I attain greater productivity in an alternative undertaking?" It is highly probable that the response to this query would be affirmative.

When I initially commenced my remote work and writing endeavors, I held a firm belief that I would thoroughly enjoy the idea of working alongside the pool, basking under the sun to acquire a bronzed complexion. Unfortunately, reality proved otherwise. The strong radiance emitted by the sun caused considerable hindrance in accomplishing my tasks on the computer, consequently compelling me to search for a more conducive setting. The most valuable counsel I can offer on this matter is to make a concerted effort to minimize any factors that may divert your attention. This will significantly enhance the ease of achieving your objectives.

Continuously strive for enhancement

It is evident that you are making substantial progress by merely having engaged in reading this book. Individuals who achieve success consistently strive for self-improvement without cessation. Whether it entails engaging in intellectual pursuits such as reading literature, participating in educational workshops, maintaining a consistent fitness regimen, or any other endeavor that fosters personal development, it is incumbent upon us to continually strive for self-improvement.

Tony Robbins espouses the belief that "the cessation of personal growth is akin to embarking on a path of decline and decay." This assertion, while forceful, holds true and bears factual weight. On a daily basis, it is essential to continually challenge oneself with increasing intensity. Acquire fresh knowledge, endeavor to approach tasks using alternative methods to those employed previously, and challenge yourself to elevate your level of accomplishment.

The Significance of Strategic Planning

Possessing a planner or a calendar facilitates gaining a comprehensive overview of your entire life. Each morning, upon arising, you are met with a clear view of the numerous prospects awaiting your endeavors. Additionally, it assists in the preservation of your morning rituals and other beneficial practices. By utilizing a planner, individuals can effectively outline and allocate specific time frames to list and pursue their desired goals. It is crucial to possess a comprehensive strategy when embarking on any endeavor in life. Developing a strategic course of action alleviates apprehension and provides a clear path to pursue. Regard a planner as a navigational guide on your journey towards enhanced productivity.

Which Should Be Utilized: Paper Planners or Digital Planners?

Prior to commencing utilization of a planner, it is imperative to ascertain and acquire a planner that suits your daily requirements optimally. I have a profound appreciation for the extent to which technology has transformed our society and given rise to numerous groundbreaking advancements. In light of my personal experiences, I have observed that paper planners exhibit a higher level of efficacy in comparison to their digital counterparts, including web-based planners and electronic calendars. Although it may not directly pertain to the genuineness of the tactile experience of paper (admittedly to a certain extent), there is a certain satisfaction in manually transcribing one's thoughts onto a physical sheet of paper. Contrast that with the action of tapping one's fingers on a touch screen or utilizing automated lists.

According to scientific research, there is evidence to support the notion that individuals are more inclined to dedicate themselves to their goals or tasks when they physically transcribe them onto a sheet of paper as opposed to recording them on a digital screen. It may appear unconventional, yet it is worth considering. Engaging in written text on a physical medium enhances cognitive function and facilitates improved retention of information. This prompts regular contemplation of one's objectives or duties.

One additional significant advantage that certain individuals might fail to recognize is the aspect of data security. It is decidedly prudent to retain information in hard copy format as opposed to entrusting it to a digital medium. In the event of an unforeseen occurrence affecting your digital planner, such as corruption, the significant amount of time and effort invested in organizing and outlining your plans over the years may be lost in a matter of seconds. Conversely, in the event that you possess a tangible planner within your bedroom, there is no cause for concern regarding the potential misplacement of your annual accomplishments and planned objectives.

Additionally, paper planners offer a greater degree of flexibility for expressing your ideas and engaging in creative planning. You will not have the privilege of experiencing such freedom on a digital platform, wherein you may encounter difficulties in locating sufficient space for data input. By utilizing a paper planner, one can effectively foster creativity and enhance the depth of their thoughts and plans. Moreover, this medium allows for the unhindered expression of ideas, including sketches and doodles, as the available space on multiple sheets of paper ensures an uninterrupted repository for one's imaginative concepts. It provides a more comprehensive perspective to analyze the clutter and identify the key activities and objectives.

Paper planners have the potential to offer greater advantages over an extended duration. It enhances one's concentration as it minimizes external disruptions. In contrast to digital planners, which can be characterized by the potential distraction posed by an abundance of social media notifications. In due course, your attentiveness will wane, leading you to overlook your intended objectives. Based on my personal expertise, a notable advantage of digital planners lies in their ability to automate recurring events and provide frequent reminders. In addition to this, paper planners appear to possess a greater sense of authenticity (pardon my tendency to be sentimental) and exhibit enhanced efficacy over the course of time.

Please remain unperturbed if circumstances deviate from the intended course.

In actuality, circumstances frequently deviate from our desired outcomes. Inevitably, we deviate from our initial ideas as we had envisaged. I desired to bring this to your attention in order to prevent you from being overly critical of yourself in the event that you are unable to execute specific projects according to your meticulously devised plans. The process of planning is both enjoyable and entails a high level of creativity. Execution presents a distinct matter. Instances may arise wherein unpredictable circumstances arise and disrupt our schedule, or we fall short of accomplishing a given task within a designated timeframe. Nevertheless, persist ceaselessly and strive to attain your aspirations. Employ a planner as an initial instrument to steer and facilitate the attainment of all those objectives. Please venture forth and acquire the planner that will serve as a repository for your accomplishments and cherished memories. Please ensure that you keep it within close proximity and refer to your tangible evidence as a valid testament of your diligent efforts and promising prospects for future accomplishments.

Planner Activity: Assume the Role of the Curator of Your Life

What factors can influence the level of satisfaction derived from utilizing a planner? This inquiry leads us to our second challenge or exercise presented in this book. You excel in an environment that inspires and fosters a sense of well-being within you. Likewise, the same principle is applicable to your planner. Upon acquiring a planner, your initial task should revolve around customizing its layout to ensure ease and comfort in its utilization. It could entail conceptualizing an exceptional cover for your planner, or fabricating innovative templates to encompass your ideas. The objective is to tailor the planner to suit your preferences, leading to an enhanced user experience. In order to derive pleasure from a mundane task such as this, it is imperative to establish certain guidelines in your schedule to ensure that it adheres to your preferences. Discover novel approaches to enhance the user experience and infuse your planner with a heightened sense of joy. Additionally, conduct thorough online research to identify various categories of planners, and subsequently select the one that aligns best with your preferences and offers optimal convenience and advantage during its usage.

Time Saving Habits

If one continuously halts their ongoing tasks to address unexpected disruptions, it not only disrupts the cohesive progression of the work, but also engenders further implications. It encroaches upon your time. The following section of the book encompasses the recommended practices that are conducive to time-saving, thereby affording you ample time to address your necessary tasks. By adhering to these guidelines, you will discover that it enables you to allocate more time effectively, thereby preventing excessive stress.

Employ the utilization of lists.

These tools serve as reminders to facilitate task completion or prompt you to recall items on your grocery list. Though there are individuals who possess a disdain for lists, the concept behind them holds merit. After one has transcribed their thoughts onto paper, they are likely to retain and recall information more effectively. Therefore, lists are recommended for the following purposes: "

- Required tasks for the day
- Essential purchases to be made (objectives during shopping)
- Schedule meetings for the upcoming day (make necessary preparations in advance)

By establishing a routine of creating itemized inventories, you will discover that daily proceedings become more manageable. Moreover, you can meticulously review these inventories to ensure that you possess all required items in advance, thereby eliminating any potential morning delays.

Ensure that everything has its designated place.

This habit makes sense. If one simply indiscriminately disperses papers upon receipt, it is improbable that such actions will contribute significantly to productivity. You must possess the capability to locate items promptly as required, and this encompasses the subsequent constituents:

- Allocate a designated area for storing your car keys and house keys.

- Establish a designated location where your paperwork can be organized and stored in labeled containers.

- Please ensure that you tidy up and stow away any items that you have used.

This can also provide utility within the office environment; therefore, it is important not to overlook its potential benefits. Once you have attended to a document or an item on your checklist, mark it as completed and then neatly file the document in the designated tray. It is truly gratifying to witness the culmination of your daily efforts consolidated in a single location, allowing you the opportunity to allocate a brief period of time to neatly organize and stow away all the contents within that receptacle.

Acquire the skill of distributing the tasks evenly amongst team members.

When one acquires the ability to delegate tasks effectively or to collaborate within a team setting, it facilitates the conservation of time, as fellow team members actively contribute to shared projects. That implies the necessity of determining the most suitable individuals for each task, and it is not a deficiency if one is unable to accomplish everything. Indeed, if that were to occur, it would likely engender discontent among individuals who genuinely desire to offer assistance or expand their knowledge. Disseminate the knowledge as it will reduce your stress levels and enable you to delegate tasks in case of unforeseen circumstances. In the context of your residence, it is encouraged to distribute both the domestic tasks and obligations among the individuals living therein. Do not shoulder the entire burden alone, but adopt a distinct allocation of responsibilities. Creating a comprehensive household chore schedule can prove instrumental in providing guidance to children and effectively distributing domestic responsibilities among cohabitants. This facilitates time-saving for all individuals involved.

Please take note of the available time slots.

This implies the allocation of a designated duration to each task within your workload. This promotes self-discipline and ensures timely completion of tasks. If you adjust your deadlines slightly, you will consistently complete your tasks within the allotted time. The issue at hand is that individuals often engage in procrastination, under the impression that they possess an ample amount of time to complete their tasks. Nevertheless, by imposing tighter deadlines, it affords one the opportunity to allocate ample time for contemplation once the task is completed, thereby enabling the pursuit of perfection or conducting a thorough review to ensure comprehensive coverage. Your time holds significance not just within the confines of these walls. Maintain a schedule and present it during the morning meal to enable each family member to contribute with their respective plans, minimizing unexpected surprises. This enables efficient retrieval of important information pertaining to family members, thereby saving valuable time otherwise spent in searching. Ensure that there is a designated front pocket on your calendar for the purpose of securely storing any papers or documents associated with the appointments displayed on said calendar.

Ensure productive utilization of meetings

Frequently, individuals attend meetings and question the purpose of allocating time to such gatherings. Please exercise caution in selecting only the meetings that pertain to the advancement of your work. In the event that something is not pertinent or if you have pressing matters to attend to, you may politely inquire about the possibility of obtaining a written account of the meeting, as reviewing minutes typically requires just five minutes to comprehend, as opposed to potentially wasting an hour in an unengaging meeting.

Develop the practice of expressing your thoughts through writing.

Individuals tend to overlook or fail to remember certain matters due to their omission from their written inventory or record. As soon as a thought arises concerning an item you require for purchase, promptly append it to your inventory. In the event that you do not possess any physical writing materials, you may alternatively input the necessary information as a memo on your mobile device. This way, once you regain access to your task list, you will have ensured that no items have been overlooked. By transferring the content from the memo to a formal list format, you will streamline your organizational process and ultimately save valuable time. This principle is applicable across all facets of your life, encompassing even your residential acquisitions. In envisioning the prospect of returning to the store due to an oversight, one can apprehend the substantial loss of precious domestic hours. Indeed, the time one spends within the confines of their residence holds equivalent significance to their professional commitments, a fact acknowledged by multitudes.

Optimizing Your Daily Routine to Enhance Productivity

If you have adhered to a set routine and grown weary of its monotony, it is now opportune to introduce changes to the status quo. There exist numerous strategies through which one can establish a foundation for daily achievements. Whether you opt to transcribe your list manually or employ the use of a computing device, a myriad of alternatives exist to facilitate a change in your approach. Engage in a variety of trials to determine the most effective approach for your specific needs.

Here are several strategies you can employ to effectively organize your day and maintain its ample level of stimulation:

Individuals who engage in freelance work and have the privilege of flexible scheduling are in a fortunate position. You are granted the freedom to pursue your preferences while ensuring timely submission of your assignments.

Please refrain from attempting to abruptly alter your established routine. It would be advisable to implement minor, uncomplicated modifications.

If you aspire to experience a sense of contentment and efficacy, it would be prudent to engage in uncomplicated endeavors, such as dedicating oneself to pursuing a singular objective each day, as a means to enhance one's motivation.

A comprehensive regimen considers not only work commitments, but also encompasses relaxation, physical activity, and dietary habits.

Endeavor to stimulate yourself by mentally visualizing your tasks as opposed to transcribing or jotting them down.

To enhance the productivity of your mornings, it is advisable to prioritize engaging in stimulating activities before delving into your emails.

The prevailing approach entails organizing your daily routine based on chronological increments. This entails determining which time of day - evening, afternoon, or morning - is most conducive to optimal productivity for you. After discovering it, remain steadfastly committed to it.

If you are not prepared to relinquish your customary routine, commence by making minor adjustments, such as reorganizing your task list in an alternative manner, in order to ascertain the most effective approach for your needs.

Planning Your Day

I hereby present a series of measures I undertake to organize my daily activities:

Please make a list of all the tasks you need to complete.

There are various means at your disposal, such as an application, the traditional method of pen and paper, a journal, or any other preferable option that suits your needs. Please document all of the tasks that you are required to complete. You may adhere to your weekly schedule, but consider incorporating additional events and tasks that may arise throughout the week when devising your daily agenda.

Here is an illustration of a typical day:

Daily morning regimen

Exercise

Engage in reading activities for a period of 30 minutes.

Consume a maximum of 2500 calories for the duration of the day.

Go for a leisurely stroll.

Compose a blog post

Create and publish a blog post

Conduct interviews with prospective candidates.

Contact the contractor to request a formal quotation.

Please contact my mother.

Arrange a gathering with acquaintances.

Express gratitude through written correspondence.

Please proceed to attend the yoga class.

I would like to accomplish these tasks throughout the day. It is possible to observe that the items are dispersed and lack an orderly arrangement. While this approach may be effective for certain individuals, it is crucial that it aligns with your own needs and requirements. If one is required to transcribe tasks in the sequence of their execution, this is the procedure for compiling a list.

It is imperative that you possess knowledge of the anticipated outcome.

What do you want? This is the paramount inquiry that necessitates your attention. You may desire to engage in physical activity today, but are you solely motivated to do so merely for the sake of claiming that you have? The purpose of the exercise must be to achieve a specific objective or result. The majority of individuals engage in physical exercise to enhance muscular strength, sustain vitality, and promote overall well-being.

This is the reason why it is imperative to have a clear understanding of your intended outcome or objective. Here is a formulation that reflects my intended outcome: "I intend to actively contribute towards achieving the successful merger between our company and the new organization." I am actively striving to achieve that objective. Given your newfound objective, you can explore alternative undertakings that could facilitate its attainment.

Understand the objective and rationale behind your desire.

When you have figured out what you want and have it written in your journal, now you must write the reasons why you want it. Please provide a detailed analysis beneath your objectives delineating the reasons for desiring this outcome. If time is a constraint, it may be convenient for you to simply jot down a handful of concise bullet points.

The aforementioned reasons will act as the driving force, inspiring and propelling you towards attaining your objective. Effort should be made to provide concise justifications so as to avoid excessive time consumption and prevent disruption to your morning activities. Whilst you engage in the act of transcribing these thoughts, you may experience a surge of motivation, instilling a sense of anticipation to embark upon your daily endeavors and initiate decisive actions.

Develop a strategic course of action

Once you have attained clarity regarding your objectives and the underlying motivations driving them, it is imperative to strategize and develop a comprehensive plan of action. This involves the process of compiling all of the written material and arranging it systematically in accordance with each of your objectives.

Suppose you intend to focus on your exercise regimen today. Allow me to present a proposed arrangement for structuring your day:

Please proceed to the fitness center.

Engage my upper limbs" or "Exercise my biceps and triceps

Consume a maximum of 2500 calories today.

Attend the yoga class.

Engage in a leisurely stroll.

Prepare and consume a nutritious beverage.

Please take the dog for a stroll around the neighborhood before retiring for the night.

Having identified your objective, it is now possible to incorporate additional elements that will enhance and expedite your progress towards said goal.

Enhanced strategic planning and efficient organization

Engaging in these activities proves to be more efficient than a conventional task list. It entails devising a strategic blueprint for the day, intended to inspire and satisfy you upon achieving your objective.

To elaborate further, it is imperative to carefully arrange and allocate time for the execution of these tasks. One can utilize a mobile calendar application to meticulously plan and allocate tasks according to their respective deadlines. Make sure to meticulously plan your day, including incorporating scheduled time for necessary phone calls.

By creating a schedule, you will attain precise awareness of the anticipated timing of events. It is not advisable to procrastinate on tasks or commitments by relying on the vague notion of "whenever I have the time", as we are all aware that unexpected events or obligations can quickly consume our schedules.

Utilize the power of leverage in your approach.

Please consider strategies for externalizing operations and capitalizing on opportunities to delegate responsibilities, if feasible. The crux of the matter lies in employing clever strategies rather than exerting excessive effort. One viable option you could consider is engaging the services of freelancers or assistants, who could expedite your progress towards achieving your objectives. This has the potential to significantly simplify your life. You will have the opportunity to concentrate on the key areas in which your expertise excels.

Resources and Applications for Enhancing Personal Organization

Amidst the myriad of tasks, scheduled commitments, engagements, and professional obligations, a sense of unease and haste pervades the majority of individuals. Frequently, our smartphones serve as the foremost source of distraction, thereby intensifying the busyness of our day. Nevertheless, your mobile device has the potential to optimize your life, contingent upon its usage. You are able to utilize the following resources to effectively manage and monitor your time usage, receive timely notifications, and cultivate more productive routines. Allow me to illustrate the potential of transforming your phone into a tool that greatly enhances efficiency and saves valuable time:

Pocket

The online labyrinth represents a significant source of wasted time. When you come across a narrative that appears captivating, refrain from immediate perusal. Instead, employ Pocket as a means to preserve it for future reference and revisit it at a more opportune moment.

Pocket provides users with the opportunity to bookmark articles for later access while conducting online browsing activities. You have the ability to categorize the videos and articles you have amassed, enabling convenient retrieval whenever you desire. After saving items to Pocket, the application will commence suggesting articles that may pique your interest.

Utilizing this application, individuals can conveniently engage in reading activities even in situations where an internet connection is not accessible. Pocket possesses the functionality to store articles for offline access, enabling you to peruse them without an internet connection. If the application is installed on multiple devices, it will synchronize all of them.

List of Habits

Their slogan is "cultivate personal growth," and this application will assist you in achieving that objective. It will assist you in making more informed decisions, such as diligently reviewing your documentation on a regular basis.

To utilize the application, simply document a series of accomplishments within the calendar or establish a routine for recurring habits. Subsequently, this application will provide you with reminders regarding the tasks that require your attention. Moreover, it will provide you with a progress report, enabling you to assess the ongoing status of this endeavor. The interface of the application is straightforward and conducive to maintaining focus. Every morning, it shall exhibit a comprehensive compilation of your daily assignments. In order to cultivate a variety of habits, a fee of $5 will be required. Although Habit List is exclusively designed for iOS, Android users can still access an equivalent application called Habit Streak.

Todoist

This application is widely regarded as the preeminent choice for managing one's task inventory. This tool is compatible with all platforms, possesses an intuitive and visually appealing interface, and boasts advanced functionalities for those who require them.

This will afford you the opportunity to establish priorities among various tasks. One could organize tasks by grouping them together, enabling the ability to maintain a distinction between personal and work-related items. "For frequently recurring tasks, such as bill payments, you can schedule them to occur on a regular basis." Should you have tasks on a weekly basis, rest assured that Todoist will not fail to remember them.

You have the option to utilize this application at no cost, or alternatively, you have the opportunity to enhance your experience by subscribing to our premium plan at the modest price of $29 per annum. With the enhancement, you have the ability to solicit prompts contingent upon your location and time, inherent backups, as well as visual representations in the form of charts illustrating your accomplishments.

Intelligent Timing

To effectively enhance the organization of your life, it is imperative to have a comprehensive understanding of how you allocate your time. This application aims to assist users in accomplishing precisely that objective. It has the capability to autonomously monitor and record your activities. You will be responsible for manually organizing and tracking your schedule, while the application will endeavor to address any idle periods throughout the day by leveraging the insights derived from your phone's sensors, which capture your past behavioral patterns. Rapid motion may indicate that you engaged in a morning jog.

Once data input is initiated into this application, it will generate comprehensive reports encompassing various aspects such as time utilization and the applications allocated to specific time intervals. If you seek to introduce variation, it is possible to generate personalized objectives that Smarter Time will assist you in attaining.

This application is exclusive to Android users at present; however, the developers are diligently working on creating a beta version compatible with iOS devices. To obtain a more precise report or additional data, it is recommended to upgrade to a plus account, which incurs a monthly price ranging from $3 to $10.

Trello

This application has garnered substantial renown as a collaborative tool utilized by teams to facilitate cohesive project management. The application's flexibility makes it highly suitable for both families and individuals, enhancing its effectiveness. It has the capacity to be modified for multiple purposes, encompassing the monitoring of diverse objectives.

Both web and mobile applications are employable, and their functionalities are entirely analogous. You generate multiple 'cards' and insert them into designated columns. Each card possesses the capacity to represent a household duty, an item on your agenda, or an imminent significant celebration. These columns have the potential to represent a multitude of elements such as dates, levels of priority, tasks, or other factors that can be utilized to organize your cards effectively.

Once you have established the method for organizing your cards, you may proceed to embellish each card with designs to facilitate their maintenance. One could potentially employ the utilization of a tinted adhesive marker, provide a concise overview, explicitly designate individuals for notification, or establish specific timelines for task completion. Subsequently, you will engage in collaborative work by offering comments, appending files, and transitioning cards across columns. The configuration can vary from uncomplicated to highly intricate.

For personal use, one can utilize its complimentary level. Businesses have the option to pay a monthly fee ranging from $10 to $21 in order to enhance the integration with other applications that you might utilize.

Cortana

In contemporary times, the majority of cellular devices are equipped with a digital assistant. Although Siri or Google Assistant are commonly relied upon by most individuals, Cortana may prove to be advantageous, particularly in instances where one engages with numerous devices or possesses a Windows 10 computer. Simply download the application in order to proceed. Subsequently, you shall proceed with the authentication process on your Microsoft account and grant her permission to organize and structure your daily affairs.

Cortana has the ability to establish task reminders, generate lists, and capture notes. When a reminder is established, it will prompt notifications at various intervals throughout the day or upon reaching a predetermined location. One could receive a notification to purchase a bouquet of flowers for their significant other while traversing their preferred floral boutique. One can schedule recurring reminders to ensure regular weekly notifications.

Cortana is compatible with a wide range of calendars, including those offered by Microsoft, Apple, and Google, that facilitate the creation of new events and enable users to view upcoming appointments. Cortana has the capability to provide you with up-to-date information regarding weather forecasts and current events.

Google Keep" Another option could be: "The digital application known as Google Keep

To commence, you will require a suitable application wherein you can compile and organize your disparate notes, lists, and jottings. Google Keep boasts a user-friendly interface and exhibits compatibility with multiple platforms.

Furthermore, Google Keep offers a multitude of organizational options in addition to its note storage functionality. One could employ consistent tags or color-coding to categorize interconnected entries. This feature facilitates the categorization of items based on their relevance to categories such as "children," "work," or "home." It possesses the capability to store checklists, hand-drawn scribbles, images, and voice recordings.

One could collaborate with other individuals who utilize Google Keep by sharing notes and transforming them into a Google Docs file, thereby achieving a more refined and professional presentation.

Crucial Time Management Skills To Achieve Workplace Success

Delegation

Task allocation is a crucial strategy for efficient time management, which can lead to significant time savings.
If you are a business owner or a manager seeking enhanced outcomes in terms of productivity improvement, it would be prudent to take into serious consideration the usage of Planner. Planner is an innovative project management tool that empowers organizations to effectively handle tasks, projects, and collaborative efforts.

Stop Procrastinating
Procrastination constitutes the act of evading a specific issue rather than actively resolving it. Regrettably, evading your inquiries today will

inexorably result in awakening to a fresh array of obstacles tomorrow.

Prioritizing Tasks

It is imperative that you provide proper training to your staff in terms of developing a comprehensive task management system, which includes instructing them on the creation of a to-do list, as well as teaching them the skills to effectively categorize and prioritize tasks based on their urgency and significance. The Eisenhower matrix exhibits substantial efficacy in assisting individuals with task prioritization.

The presence of freedom will enhance productivity and foster innovation.
Certain employees excel at undertaking challenging tasks, while others demonstrate optimal performance when

commencing their duties in the middle phase.

Grant your employees the autonomy to organize and express their true selves, while still ensuring prompt completion of their tasks.

Incentivize yourself and your staff members

Implementing a system of incentivization for your employees, either through the provision of small rewards or the encouragement for self-compensation, will serve as a considerable catalyst for motivating them to achieve optimal efficiency and timeliness in their job performance.

Receiving recognition is universally appreciated, and this gesture will greatly enhance overall morale.

Establish objectives for managing time.

Place your attention on eradicating activities that consume time unnecessarily and enhancing efficiency through the implementation of motivational techniques and effective time management strategies. By doing so, you will consistently ensure that deadlines, provided they are rational and attainable, are met.

Nothing Happens Overnight

A multitude of individuals will peruse this literary work and harbor the notion that they will effectuate a myriad of transformations, believing that an imminent alteration will transpire in the coming days. I regret to inform you that the outcome you anticipate is not going to transpire as you hope. You will need to invest effort into this task. This outcome cannot be expected simply by perusing a book and desiring its occurrence. It is imperative that you ensure its execution. Where do you commence the process?

21. To commence, it is imperative that you initiate with a meticulously planned schedule, followed by an earnest examination of your life as detailed in this book. Select a single

recommendation that you deem to be highly efficacious and proceed with implementing the suggested modifications. As an illustration, should you find yourself lacking sufficient sleep, as previously mentioned, prioritize the resolution of this issue as your primary objective. Upon addressing that matter, you shall proceed to another realm, namely motivation and incentives.

You may discover that various recommendations provided in this book are interconnected, thus emphasizing the utmost importance of concurrently implementing and integrating these suggestions. Equally significant is the avoidance of attempting to alter an excessive amount of elements simultaneously. For instance, while it is true that increasing one's productivity is possible by waking up earlier in the morning, it is also true that maintaining a healthy diet and engaging in regular exercise significantly contribute to this goal. Furthermore, the recommendations provided in this book will undoubtedly assist in achieving desired outcomes. Nevertheless, attempting to implement all these changes simultaneously will inevitably lead to total failure. Consider the matter from this perspective. When engaging in mountain climbing, it is imperative to meticulously strategize the placement of each step you take. In order to reach your destination, it is essential to proceed gradually by taking measured strides. Engaging in hasty and excessive multitasking will inevitably result in failure. This applies to all aspects of life as well.

22. This leads me to the pursuit of a lifestyle that encompasses optimal well-being and vitality. Let us commence our discussion by addressing the matter of your dietary intake. Excessive

consumption of food or the consumption of foods that induce lethargy can significantly hinder one's productivity. Alternatively, should you choose to consume nourishing foods that enhance bodily functions and stimulate vitality, you will considerably enhance your productivity and accomplish tasks more effectively.

23. I would like to now address the topic of physical activity. A significant number of individuals fail to comprehend how the inclusion of an additional task to one's pre-existing list would contribute to enhanced productivity. However, I implore you to persist with me in exploring this concept. It is imperative to ensure that you are engaging in sufficient physical activity as your mental well-being is closely linked to your physical well-being. Engaging in a predominantly inactive lifestyle and neglecting one's physical well-being can

potentially result in the development of depression. Granting oneself the opportunity to succumb to despondency will inevitably breed further inclination towards procrastination, exacerbating the overarching predicament of depression. Engaging in regular physical activity and maintaining good physical health will result in increased energy levels, thereby reducing the propensity to procrastinate on important tasks.

It is imperative that you bear in mind the utmost importance of prioritizing self-care. Failure to prioritize self-care will impede your ability to assist others in fulfilling their expectations of you. This encompasses your duties both in the professional sphere and within the domestic realm. Engaging in regular physical activity can enhance your overall daily productivity, as it serves as a source of motivation and promotes a heightened sense of self-esteem.

Consequently, it additionally aids in surmounting any self-doubt or apprehension of failure that one may be grappling with.

24. Eliminate from your life any elements that do not serve to bestow benefits upon you. On multiple occasions, we tend to procrastinate on tasks that we acknowledge as necessary until the final moments due to a sense of being overwhelmed. Compose a comprehensive inventory of all the factors within your life that are consuming your valuable time. Once you have compiled a comprehensive inventory, it is necessary to generate a roster enumerating the top three paramount aspects that you hold dear in your life. Now, proceed to review your catalog and identify the activities in which you actively engage, thereby promoting and upholding these

principles. Do you observe all that remains? Get rid of it.

The aforementioned principle also holds true in regard to individuals. Allow me to recount a narrative. There were individuals who would routinely appear at my residence without any prior invitation. They would never make an attempt to contact me or inquire about my availability. It had reached a stage wherein they would arrive prior to my rising from bed and linger until considerably after dinner. Although it is not within my nature to exhibit unkindness towards others, I must admit that this situation has increasingly provoked my irritation. They were well aware of my ongoing workload. I made an attempt to engage in work activities while they were present in my residence, however, this endeavor merely resulted in their subsequent attempts to persuade me that there existed a more efficient approach to accomplishing the task at hand. When the situation escalated, I found it necessary to communicate to these individuals that if they were unable to demonstrate respect for my personal life, my privacy, and my professional endeavors, they would no longer be welcome in my residence.

Presently, these individuals no longer frequent this vicinity. Do I miss them? Honestly no. I greatly appreciate solitude, as it allows me to concentrate exclusively on matters of personal significance. There are occasions when it becomes necessary to prioritize one's personal needs and values over those of others, and this frequently entails distancing oneself from certain individuals.

25. Cease your perpetual pursuit of flawlessness. I am familiar with the

experience of desiring to execute every task with utmost perfection. You should commence engaging in practical thinking. Is it imperative that every aspect remains flawless throughout the entirety of each day?

26. Please refrain from chastising yourself should you encounter failure. As previously mentioned, it is crucial to acknowledge that this process will not occur instantaneously. It is imperative that you refrain from self-criticism each time an error is made. In the event of failure, make another attempt. Eventually you will succeed. It required a span of 6 months for me to attain success, and it continues to be a pursuit on which I dedicate myself daily.

27. Divide the tasks into more manageable projects. If you encounter a project that appears to be overwhelming, it would be beneficial to

decompose it into more manageable components. As an illustration, when engaging in household cleaning tasks, it is imperative to approach each room methodically, focusing on one area and task at a time. If you happen to find yourself engaged in multiple tasks simultaneously, simply take a moment to consciously acknowledge this fact. You will be able to achieve greater productivity by concentrating on a single task at any given time.

28. Acquire the ability to identify the initiation of procrastination. By diligently observing, one will discern a prevailing sensation, behavior, or thought pattern that typically occurs when initiating the act of procrastination. It was at the commencement of the month that I ascertained the complete settlement of all my financial obligations for the subsequent duration of 30 days. By the

conclusion of the second week, I began to sense the imminent rush to undertake the same tasks once more. I acquired the ability to discern this pattern, and despite having developed a tendency to procrastinate at the start of each month, I exerted even more effort during that period to accomplish as much as possible. I made a personal commitment to exert maximum effort during the initial portion of the month, with the understanding that despite continuing my work until the month's conclusion, I would achieve a significantly higher level of relaxation compared to my previous state. Consequently, I can affirm that this objective has been successfully accomplished.

29. Direct your attention to the desired outcome. Contemplate the objective you are striving to achieve. Are you, like myself, making diligent efforts to fulfill your financial obligations? It is possible

that the ultimate outcome could be a tidy abode that provides you with contentment, or the cultivation of exquisite blossoms in the vicinity which offer you great delight. Maintain unwavering concentration on achieving whatever goal you are currently striving for. Maintaining focused attention on your objective will assist in preventing future instances of procrastination.

30. Delegate. If there are additional individuals within your familial network who can provide support in achieving your objectives, it is advisable to begin the process of assigning tasks and responsibilities to them. Children have the ability to tidy their beds, organize their toys, manage dishware, and contribute to household chores such as laundry. It is crucial for you to comprehend that undertaking everything independently is unfeasible;

thus, it is advisable to commence seeking assistance.

Leveraging Your Task List For Establishing Goals And Deadlines

What are the reasons for establishing goals and implementing strict timelines? What advantages will this offer you? A goal is an objective that one aspires to accomplish in the forthcoming period. It has the potential to be either a brief or extended timeframe, and may entail something as straightforward as desiring punctuality in commuting to work. Without a clear objective in mind, one's progress will remain stagnant, resulting in an inability to make any headway. The difference between arriving at work 10 minutes late or 30 minutes late would be of no significance to you. You will persist in navigating life without a clear sense of direction or purpose. However, by setting objectives that you aspire to accomplish within a specific timeframe, you will imbue your daily routine with a profound sense of direction. The feeling of purpose will drive you to establish additional objectives as you encounter the gratification that comes from effectively finishing the tasks outlined on your agenda.

Employing your task agenda as a means to establish objectives and time limits proves to be a beneficial approach in dissecting grander aspirations into feasible tasks. There are numerous objectives in one's life that cannot be feasibly achieved within a 24-hour period, particularly for individuals who lead the life of a typical person, and even more so for those who are working mothers. There are occasions when it is not feasible to complete the tasks of writing bills and updating the checkbook within the constraints of a single day's to-do list. It might be necessary for you to carefully document the financial obligations on the initial day. It may be necessary to record the receipts in the checkbook on the second day. Additionally, on the third day, it may be necessary to revise the balance recorded in the checkbook. It is contingent upon the other activities one is aware of that must be accomplished during the day, as well as being cognizant of one's time constraints. If you happen to have a scheduled scholastic event on the very evening you intend to settle the bills, it would be prudent to avoid placing undue pressure on yourself. Repetitive setbacks can gradually erode one's self-esteem and potentially lead to the abandonment of goal-oriented pursuits. Don't forgo sleep. Insufficient sleep will compromise your objectives for the following day, thereby precipitating an unpropitious cycle of ineffectiveness and irritability.

Furthermore, there exist objectives that cannot be accomplished within a single diurnal period. It is not feasible to complete your degree within the timeframe of a single day. Except in the circumstance that occurs on the day of graduation, where the only task required is to remain at home until the diploma is received. Yet, it remains beyond your control to dictate the precise timing of the diploma's delivery via postal services. If you seek tangible evidence of your degree attainment on that specific day, attending the ceremony becomes necessary, entailing the completion of various pre-requisites prior to the commencement of the ceremonial proceedings, culminating in the moment of crossing the stage and receiving the certificate.

Even a comparatively minor undertaking, such as tidying my basement, may still prove unattainable within a single day, when juxtaposed with the significant accomplishment of completing your degree. In the absence of an available vacation day, considering that the children will be present in the evening, and with personal regard for the importance of restful sleep (which I have sorely missed), it appears highly improbable to accomplish such an overwhelming task without dividing it into more manageable portions. Certain individuals may hold the perception that this statement is an overstatement. You are yet to behold the state of my basement! Within its 1800 square feet confines, two storage lockers have been crammed, alongside an abundance of half-unclosed boxes, disgorging their contents onto the neglected, dusty floor.

The initial action you must take entails identifying the objective you aim to achieve. After the establishment of the objective, proceed to systematically decompose it into identifiable and executable tasks that must be accomplished in order to achieve the desired outcome. For goals with a far-reaching scope, it will be necessary to further dissect those actionable steps into a series of smaller, more manageable steps. Once all of those items are thoroughly analyzed, you will be able to discern the tasks that can be completed on a daily basis in order to attain the said goal in subsequent periods. Every task accomplished from your checklist will propel you further towards your ultimate objective.

By decomposing your goals into manageable daily tasks, you can avoid surrendering to your aspirations prematurely, denying yourself the opportunity to thrive.

Key Take Always:

• Some objectives may require more than a single day to accomplish. • Certain goals cannot be achieved within a 24-hour timeframe. • There exist ambitions that cannot be realized within a single day. Employing your task agenda as a means to establish objectives and timeframes is an advantageous approach to decompose lofty objectives into feasible tasks.

• After determining a desired objective, it is advisable to disassemble that goal into manageable, concrete tasks that must be successfully executed to ultimately achieve the target.

• Each day, endeavor to pinpoint one task that can be completed to aid in your future goal attainment.

Overcoming Procrastination

Do not defer the tasks that demand your immediate attention and let procrastination hijack your precious time. Remember to always seize the present moment as the opportune time for taking action. Exert a greater amount of effort to overcome the habit of procrastination and uncover the objectives that must be accomplished.

An effective strategy to overcome procrastination is to educate yourself you are simply going to embark on a project for a couple of minutes, say ten minutes. Once you commence your duties, your capacity for imaginative thinking will be unleashed.

Subsequently, you will realize your desire to persist with the assignment and, quite possibly, see it through to its completion. The solution to overcoming procrastination can be as simple as dedicating a small portion of time to initiate tasks. That is all.

Typically, tomorrow tends to be the most hectic day of the week.
Spanish proverb: "Más vale tarde que nunca"
How swiftly does the phrase 'not now' transform into the word 'never'.
Martin Luther
In hindsight, you might regret not having commenced your endeavors today, one year hence.
Karen Lamb

One of the most prevalent dilemmas is the act of delaying or postponing tasks, commonly referred to as procrastination. Collectively, we possess an inherent understanding of our desired course of action and the obligations that lie before us. However, we tend to invest a considerable amount of time engaging in seemingly simpler tasks or seeking solace in activities such as watching television, listening to music, or browsing blogs. There is absolutely no harm in indulging in occasional moments of respite.

However, should one indulge in excessive procrastination, the vital tasks at hand may remain unaccomplished. Additionally, you will inevitably plunge into adverse cycles whenever your self-esteem diminishes, and you will find yourself immersed in a prolonged state of discontent. May I inquire about your occupation?

What is your profession? Presented herein are seven indispensable strategies to effectively overcome procrastination, thereby embarking on a more fulfilling journey towards holistic living.

1. Start doing. Quit thinking.

Overthinking the action frequently leads to its failure.

Eva Young

With a modicum of forethought, you can undoubtedly accomplish your desired goals. A significant amount of deliberation and strategizing often yields contrary outcomes.

You contemplate, hold conviction, and endeavor to formulate an optimal course of action. A strategic approach that encompasses flawlessness, zero rejection, and the absence of adversity and complications. Indeed, the existence of such a thing is non-existent. However, as long as you operate on such a plan you'll be able to protect yourself.

2. Do not disregard a job disproportionately.

If you desire to transform an uncomplicated task into a formidable endeavor, simply persist in procrastinating its completion."

Procrastinating on a straightforward task complicates matters. Delaying a difficult task renders it impracticable."

George Claude Lorimer

Through the process of excessive rumination and procrastination, one aims not only to shield oneself from anguish. You tend to exaggerate trivial matters as well. The aforementioned quotations are remarkably precise, to the point where any form of amusement is absent. The more you procrastinate and extend the hours, the more the matter becomes increasingly burdensome on your conscience.

As you occupy this space, it consequently broadens your mental capacity. And as a result of your procrastination, it is probable that you are perceiving it in a unfavorable manner. This phenomenon gives rise to a colossal Godzilla, an intimidating creature that poses a significant threat to the harmony of one's personal existence.

Devise a strategic plan before proceeding with its execution.

Frequently, there is no need for deliberate planning as one has previously encountered the situation and is cognizant of the necessary actions to undertake. Therefore, refrain from contemplation and proceed with the task at hand, irrespective of your emotions and convictions.

The current fluctuations in your emotional state are as changeable as atmospheric conditions, making them an unreliable foundation for reliable guidance or decision-making. You are not obliged to adhere to its instructions (they do not possess the rigidity of iron shackles). One must only engage in actions that are assuredly correct.

3. Simply commence by initiating the initial action.

It is unnecessary to have a full view of the entire staircase; simply initiate the process by taking the initial step."

Martin Luther King Jr, part of the esteemed and highly regarded civil rights movement,

When one begins to contemplate the distant future, alternative pursuits or vocations may seem exceedingly impracticable.

Consequently, you tend to cease operations due to feelings of being overburdened and subsequently engage in aimless internet browsing. This is among the rationales supporting the wisdom of preparing for the future, while simultaneously redirecting focus towards the present and its temporal immediacy.

Therefore, your focus should be directed towards initiating the first step at this moment. That is the sole matter you are required to direct your attention towards, without any additional considerations. Through the act of initiating, you transform your cognitive state from one of resistance to a more optimistic mindset, characterized by a sense of purpose and enthusiasm.

You place yourself in a state of heightened self-assurance and receptiveness, reaching a point where you may not be particularly eager to proceed further, but you are at least willing to embrace this initial stage. This implies the potential to proceed further and subsequently advance even more.

The critical point to consider is that the entirety of the staircase remains impervious to visual perception, as it will intermittently undergo modifications and manifests progressively during the course of ascent. Hence, it is common for program outlines to slightly deviate or shift when they are implemented. You perceive that your factual map does not align with the actual state of reality.

4. Commence by tackling the most challenging task of the day.
Prioritize the difficult tasks. The straightforward tasks will be handled without effort"
Dale Carnegie
May you perhaps have an important obligation to attend to, which you additionally worry could potentially lead to embarrassment. Perhaps you are aware that you have fallen behind with responding to your emails and currently have a substantial backlog to address. It

is possible that you still have to complete the previous five pages of your paper.

Regardless of the circumstances, prioritize tending to it as your utmost priority.

If you initiate your day in this manner, you can experience a sense of relief. You experience a sense of tranquility and self-affirmation. Furthermore, the rest of the evening, as well as your task list, tends to manifest a noticeable reduction in weight and increased ease of completion. It is remarkable the impact that this single activity has.

5. Simply make a decision. Any choice.

When facing a decisive moment, it is most prudent to opt for the most fitting course of action, as any alternative would be misguided, and the most peculiar choice would be to abstain from taking any action.

Theodore Roosevelt

We experience a sense of unease when we refrain from taking action, as it goes against our innate nature. It would be advisable to adopt a resolute demeanor and take action.

If you tend to engage in procrastination when faced with necessary tasks, but fail to take the corresponding measures required to address those obligations. In due course, an internal conflict arises.

All of your consistent actions serve as indicators that provide insights into your true character. Indeed, engaging in the practice of reciting self-affirmations that promote a sense of confidence can prove to be beneficial.

Deliberately selecting constructive behaviors, repeatedly and purposefully, fosters the development of self-assurance and cultivates a perception of oneself evolving into a person of worth.

By engaging in the act of procrastination, one significantly diminishes their sense of self-worth and inadvertently communicates to themselves that they possess a notable level of helplessness and indecisiveness.

6. Face your fear.

Procrastination can be seen as the fear of achieving success. People engage in procrastination due to their apprehension regarding the success that they anticipate achieving if they were to progress at this moment. Due to the weightiness of success, it entails a corresponding responsibility, making it considerably more convenient to indulge in procrastination and adopt the mentality of postponing tasks to a hypothetical future.

Denis Waitley

I believe that is indeed accurate. It is more convenient to subsist based on the notion of a hypothetical future. It poses a greater challenge to accomplish the task. Taking the chance of being perceived as foolish. To err and stumble is more prudent than evading such discomfort.

Opting for the more convenient option tends to provide a certain degree of comfort, a definite level of achievement, a feeling of remorse for missed opportunities, and a general sense of dissatisfaction. You contemplate the potential outcomes that could have transpired had you engaged in greater activity and embraced a wider array of opportunities.

The more challenging decision offers uncertain outcomes. However, it will undoubtedly make you feel truly alive.

7. Complete it.

Much of the anxiety experienced by individuals does not stem from having an excessive workload."

Failing to initiate the first step toward achieving a goal may lead to a negative emotional state. Nevertheless, failing to complete what one has initiated can also result in an undesirable state of distress. You genuinely experience feelings of stress or fatigue, occasionally without comprehending their underlying causes. It feels as though your inner strength has been instantly depleted.

In the event that is the circumstance, kindly review the projects and tasks in which you are presently engaged. Is there anything that you are aware of which you desire to complete but have not done so yet? Make an effort to locate that which is finished as soon as you can, which will subsequently result in a significant improvement in your overall well-being.

Just be mindful. One must not perceive it as necessary to complete all pursuits embarked upon. If a publication is of poor quality, consider selecting an alternative reading material. Using this rationale as a justification for giving up on something that appears unfamiliar or challenging is not an advisable course of action. However, there is no legislation mandating the completion of all tasks.

However, The Vast Majority Of Individuals Tend To Engage In Procrastination. Why?

Principal Factors Contributing to Procrastination

Causes for procrastination: An Analysis
What neurological mechanisms underlie the behavioral tendency to evade tasks that are known to be necessary?

PRESENT BIAS
Behavioural psychology research ascribes procrastination to the phenomenon known as "Time Inconsistency" or "Present Bias." Time inconsistency pertains to the cognitive propensity inherent in individuals to assign higher value to rewards that are received immediately, rather than those received in the future. This elucidates why individuals are often inclined

towards procrastination, despite possessing earnest intentions.

The concept of present bias asserts that our inclination towards immediate gratification or rewards outweighs our inclination towards long-term rewards. Hence, indulging in procrastination currently elicits a sense of gratification.
One can acquire a comprehensive understanding of this concept by employing the technique of envisioning oneself as having two distinct identities: the 'Present Self' and the 'Future Self'. When embarking upon the establishment of long-term objectives - such as the accumulation of 1 crore rupees for your retirement years - you are effectively strategizing for the betterment of your Future Self. You are conceptualizing the desired trajectory of your future life. Scientists have discovered that the contemplation of

one's Future Self effortlessly enables the brain to recognize and appreciate the significance of engaging in actions that yield long-term advantages. The Future Self prioritizes the attainment of rewards that have a lasting impact.

Nevertheless, while the Future Self reaps the benefits, it is solely the Present Self that possesses the ability to enact change. The endeavors and the self-imposed hardships undertaken by the current self. Once the moment to arrive at a verdict arises, you relinquish the ability to select the version of yourself that will manifest in the future. Now, you currently find yourself in the present moment, with your mind actively engaged in contemplating the Present Self. Scholars have uncovered that the Present Self exhibits a preference for immediate gratification rather than long-term rewards.

Therefore, the Present Self and the Future Self frequently find themselves in conflict. The Future Self aspires to maintain a healthy and lean physique, while the Present Self fancies indulging in a donut. Indeed, it is widely recognized that maintaining a nutritious diet in the present is imperative in order to prevent the onset of obesity a decade from now. However, the ramifications, such as a heightened susceptibility to conditions like diabetes or heart failure, will not manifest for several years. The individual who might experience the negative consequences would likely be one's future self. The prevailing sentiment of questioning the necessity to make sacrifices for the sake of a future self that seems far removed serves as a catalyst for the present self to delay engaging in any behaviors such as reducing sugar intake or committing to a regular exercise routine.

Likewise, a significant number of young individuals are cognizant of the importance of saving for retirement during their thirties and forties; however, the advantageous outcome of such endeavors may only materialize after several decades have passed. It is significantly more convenient for the Current Self to recognize the worth of purchasing a fresh pair of footwear compared to setting aside a sum of Rs.3000 for the future well-being of the 70-year-old version of oneself.

This phenomenon illustrates why individuals may retire for the night feeling inspired to enact a transformation in their lives; however, upon awakening, they invariably discover themselves reverting to antiquated behaviors. The human mind prioritizes future-oriented outcomes, particularly those that offer long-term advantages. However, it exhibits a preference for instant gratification when it pertains to present circumstances.

For example,
Mohan is an author of fictional narratives. He currently has an unfinished book and is awaiting its official publication. Notwithstanding, the immediate gratification derived from remaining in bed and indulging in television holds greater allure than the distant satisfaction derived from publishing a book, an undertaking that would undoubtedly require a significantly protracted period of time to achieve. He allocates his time before the television while the book patiently waits.
DEPRESSION

Furthermore, the act of delaying tasks can be attributed to the presence of depressive symptoms. Experiencing emotions of despair, powerlessness, and diminished vitality can pose challenges when it comes to initiating and completing even the most straightforward undertaking. Additionally, depression may give rise to feelings of uncertainty towards oneself. When faced with the predicament of being unable to determine an effective approach to a project or experiencing a sense of self-doubt regarding one's capabilities, it is plausible that deferring the task may present itself as a more convenient option.

PERFECTIONIST APPROACH:

The pursuit of perfection is the primary catalyst for delaying progress. It is imperative to consistently strive for excellence in every undertaking we embark upon. Nevertheless, striving for excellence and achieving perfection are distinct concepts. To exert utmost effort is to optimize the utilization of the time, knowledge, and resources bestowed upon us at any given moment. The fact remains that regardless of our endeavors, opportunities for future enhancements will inevitably persist. It is imperative that we acknowledge the intrinsic value of perpetual enhancement as an exquisite facet of existence.

The issue with perfectionism lies in our pursuit of achieving an ideal that is inherently unattainable. That is not possible. As we endeavor to attain a state of flawlessness, we inadvertently refrain from taking initiative, as we feel compelled to delay commencement until the pinnacle of perfection is reached. Attaining perfection is not a requisite nor indispensable. Do not expend excessive effort striving for perfection, as even in the event of an error, the valuable feedback obtained from such experiences presents a splendid occasion for learning.

According to Elizabeth Gilbert, perfectionism can be likened to a fear dressed in elegant footwear.

Perfectionism arises from the underlying apprehension of falling short of expectations.

Perfectionism can be described as an apprehension towards encountering failure. Due to the excessive self-identification of a perfectionist with errors and shortcomings.

However, committing an error or encountering a setback in one's life does not imply that one is deemed a failure. The sole path to failure lies in ceasing one's efforts, personal development, knowledge acquisition, and willingness to embrace risks.

Given that success constantly lies one stride beyond failure.

What characterizes a perfectionist? Unrealistically high standards

Perfectionists set exceptionally lofty targets, a noteworthy achievement deserving acknowledgement. Nevertheless, individuals with a propensity for perfectionism are unable to take pleasure in minor accomplishments throughout their journey. They perceive that their sense of self-validation is contingent upon accomplishing the ultimate objective. Given ambitious objectives, it does require a considerable amount of time.
The cause of their loss of motivation, tendency to procrastinate, or avoidance of action stems from the apprehension surrounding their perceived inability to attain their ambitious objectives due to

the considerable expectations they place upon themselves.

Fear of Failure

Perfectionists procrastinate very often. This can be attributed to apprehensions regarding potential failure. The stakes associated with taking risks are unacceptably high due to the fear of committing errors and experiencing a sense of inadequacy. On the contrary, individuals with perfectionistic tendencies perceive a constant need to engage in further preparation, exert more effort, and acquire additional knowledge prior to undertaking essential actions.

Nevertheless, it is an undeniable reality that this level of flawlessness remains unattainable, resulting in individuals perpetually remaining in the preparatory phase. The remedy lies in acquiring a profound and comprehensive comprehension that engaging in imperfect yet genuine actions represents the most optimal course of action.

Taking action towards a small act of kindness holds greater value than harboring lofty intentions devoid of any action. Impeccability is synonymous with well-meaning. However, an act can be considered a virtuous action.

Inner critic

The pervasive internal voice that consistently passes judgment and offers criticism towards oneself is particularly prominent among individuals with perfectionistic tendencies. This inner critic will perpetually bring to your attention instances in which you experienced failure, made errors, articulated something incorrectly, or fell short of perfection.

Overworking

Due to their perpetual pursuit of perfection, perfectionists also exhibit a propensity for excessive labor. They have the perception that they are unworthy of rest until they have attained perfection.

They are prone to disregarding essential measures for their physical, mental, and emotional wellbeing, such as adequate rest, taking a break, spending quality time with their dear ones, and so forth. They hold the belief that the greater their efforts, the higher their likelihood of achieving success, disregarding the fact that this dedication merely propels them towards an everlasting pursuit of flawlessness.

IGNORANCE

Frequently, we engage in procrastination without being aware of it. This phenomenon may arise due to a dearth of clearly defined objectives to fulfill on a daily basis, consequently causing us to be thrown off track by the multitude of tasks that come our way. The appearance of being occupied can be deceptive, as it frequently serves as a disguise for our tendency to postpone tasks. We are currently occupied with responding to emails, conducting telephone communications, and attending to various tasks; however, these activities do not contribute to our progress on matters of significance. Experiencing excessive busyness can thus serve as an indication of inefficiency in the workplace, particularly stemming from an inability to make effective judgments.

Indolence or absence of strategic planning

The inherent inclination of human beings is to reduce exertion. As a consequence, we exhibit an increased inclination to evade challenging tasks and actions. Frequently, we experience a sense of powerlessness when faced with a project that appears to be an insurmountable task, causing us to opt for avoidance. In order to address this issue, it is imperative to break down a project into minuscule tasks that may appear inconsequential. Subsequently, it is imperative to approach each of these tasks with determination and unwavering dedication.

INSUFFICIENT ASSISTANCE & COMPETITION

Engaging in employment bears resemblance to warfare, for one thrives in the presence of collaborators. In order to surmount challenging tasks, it is imperative to associate oneself with individuals who have aligned aspirations. These individuals can offer a network of support to depend on amidst challenging circumstances. Furthermore, they serve as a stimulus for self-improvement and drive your competitiveness.

LACK OF CONCENTRATION

Accomplishing tasks necessitates the utilization of three fundamental resources: time, vitality, and focus. The greater our ability to concentrate these three resources towards a unified objective, the higher the likelihood of achieving success within a particular domain. Nevertheless, our organizational effectiveness is frequently lacking, resulting in the misguided allocation of these invaluable resources necessary for attaining success. Hence, the need for occasional inventory arises. It will help establish a proper hierarchy of priorities.

Disregarding one's intuition

Additionally, there are instances when we compel ourselves to engage in activities that we find unpleasant. This incompatibility can manifest itself in various ways, encompassing the chosen occupation, the surrounding work environment, the sector of industry, and so on. When an innate sense of misalignment with one's pursuits surfaces, it becomes arduous to unleash one's utmost potential. Procrastination may also be associated with a lack of affinity towards our tasks. Frequently, individuals demonstrate persistence until a critical juncture occurs wherein they recognize their mistakes. In order to rectify this issue, it is imperative that we allocate a designated period for self-reflection on a daily basis. It is imperative to establish cognitive room to facilitate the transition of unconscious thoughts into the realm of consciousness. This can be achieved through engaging in activities such as walking, practicing meditation, playing a musical instrument, and various other pursuits.

LACK OF PURPOSE

The source of passion and enthusiasm in our lives is derived from possessing a clear understanding of our true identity and the goals we aspire to achieve. This feeling of purpose serves as the driving force behind our ability to rise each morning and confront the tasks that lie ahead. In the face of difficulty, when our aspirations are firmly established, we are compelled to persevere and accomplish the objective at hand. Even mundane and monotonous tasks can be endured. Nonetheless, in the event that we do not perceive any advantageous outcomes resulting from the task's completion, our enthusiasm for engaging in said task diminishes entirely. Consequently, we have opted to delay the commencement of said task. Engaging in procrastination appears to be the inevitable course of action, leading to the postponement of these tasks until their completion becomes imperative. Subsequently, we will continue working into the evening in order to complete the task. The overall standard of our work is compromised, leading to inconveniences for others. However, it should be noted that we have fulfilled the requested tasks to the best of our abilities.

The tenth point on the list is as follows: I am not fond of the tasks at hand.

There exists a distinction between tasks that bring us pleasure and those that elicit our aversion. It is customary for individuals to promptly attend to tasks they find favorable, while deferring those that do not hold their interest. Engaging in work that aligns with our interests alleviates the sense of labor, transforming the process into a delightful endeavor, akin to indulging in a personal pastime. We do not require any external sources of motivation to complete that task.

Nevertheless, conversely holds to be factual. If we possess a disdain towards our occupation, we perceive it as an onerous obligation. We lack the drive and would expend considerable efforts to evade accomplishing it.

Eleventhly," or "In the eleventh place," or "Moving on to number 11. Work-related fatigue and emotional exhaustion

The experience of facing pressure and overcoming challenges can lead to the optimal expression of one's abilities. Nevertheless, similar to all commendable qualities, a balanced approach is essential. Periodic intervals of rest and recovery are necessary to replenish one's energy. In the absence of these intervals of rest, one would endure incessant strain, a burden that the human body and mind are not suited to sustain over extended durations. The outcome of sustained pressure is the manifestation of stress and burnout. In the event that one is encountering burnout, a noticeable decrease in physical and mental energy may occur, leading to a heightened propensity for procrastination resulting from diminished motivation and vitality.

Twelve. Lack of prioritization skills" or "Incapacity to establish priorities

Occasionally, you tend to assume an excessive workload. You possess an aversion to declining requests, hence you willingly undertake any task put forth before you. Instead of concentrating on a single task, you attempt to satisfy everyone by shifting between different tasks. The outcome is that no progress is achieved. In due course, you find yourself confronted with an extensive agenda that evokes a sense of trepidation upon its mere observation. The prospect of finalizing the list of tasks is so daunting and distressing that one is at a loss as to where to commence. One may choose not to contemplate upon the matter, and instead engage in trivial undertakings as a means of diverting attention. This grants you the sensation of being occupied, yet yields no fruitful outcomes.

Thirteen. ANXIETY

Procrastination may ensue as a result of anxiety, stemming from apprehensions surrounding the anticipated reception of the final outcome. Perhaps there is a possibility of experiencing a loss in terms of the sale, potential ridicule from others pertaining to your presentation, and the perception of your worthlessness by your superiors, consequently bringing you closer to the prospect of dismissal. Anxiety causes individuals to concentrate intensively on the adverse potential outcomes, resulting in a perception of their actuality. One might perceive it as more prudent to refrain from attempting the task, as the potential repercussions of inadequacy could be deemed unfavorable.

Divide Larger Projects Into Smaller Components

A significant undertaking, to be completed within a defined timeframe, can be daunting; therefore, it is advisable to divide it into smaller, more feasible assignments. You only require a single sheet of paper and a pen.

Initially, accurately ascertain the aim and objectives of your project. Subsequently, compile an inventory of sequential tasks that must be undertaken in order to achieve your desired outcomes. It is advisable to also consider the required resources for those tasks.

After compiling your checklist, proceed to designate a specific time frame or deadline for each individual task, thereby emphasizing the due date for the culmination of the entire project.

In conclusion, allocate the tasks evenly over the remaining days, starting from the earliest possible time. By organizing your daily activities and realizing the presence of small tasks to be fulfilled, you will perceive the project as less burdensome in contrast to the sense of overwhelming responsibility upon waking up every morning.

Enhancing Your Ability to Make Effective Decisions

The process of decision-making is a formidable task for individuals, primarily due to the apprehension surrounding the potential consequences of making an erroneous judgement. In order to efficiently allocate time, individuals are consistently presented with the discretion to make choices regarding specific tasks, their respective timings, and the methods by which they are to be executed. The more adept you are at making decisions, the more proficient you will be in managing the time at your disposal.

In order to arrive at well-considered choices, one must first evaluate the magnitude of the decision at hand. Deliberate upon the advantages and disadvantages of each option, carefully evaluate them, and ascertain which alternative boasts a greater number of advantages in comparison to disadvantages.

Time undeniably plays a pivotal role in the process of decision-making. It is essential to take into account the remaining time at your disposal and strategize on maximizing its utilization. Additionally, there exist certain decisions that do not necessitate immediate resolution. Therefore, it is advisable to allocate an extended period of contemplation for such options.

In the event that all other options prove to be unsuccessful, resort to the action of tossing a coin. It is inconsequential which side would ultimately prevail. The crucial aspect is that you will attain clarity regarding your preferred choice once the coin has rendered its decision.

The Physical Aspect Of Time Management

This chapter will address a conspicuous but frequently disregarded element of Time Management: the state of your physical well-being.

In the preceding sections of the literature, we have thoroughly examined the factors contributing to procrastination; however, it is imperative to acknowledge that one pivotal catalyst, often cited by individuals, has been inadvertently omitted: idleness.

However, indolence is an exceedingly imprecise justification. The term "laziness" is often employed by individuals who have a tendency to procrastinate, but its meaning can be ambiguous. Frequently, there exists a fundamental underlying cause for individuals' inclination towards laziness. The examination of the initial chapters may serve as the fundamental rationale for procrastination, a phenomenon that is often incorrectly labeled as laziness.

The Phenomenon of Genuine Indolence and Effective Measures to Combat It

How would you characterize your current level of energy?

Individuals who exhibit authentic indolence, rather than engaging in mere postponement, often experience a dearth of vitality. In essence, they lack the energy required to accomplish the tasks outlined in their agenda.

Thankfully, elevating your energy level can be achieved effortlessly provided that you are willing to allocate resources towards this endeavor. Primarily, the occurrence of low energy can be ascribed to poor physical well-being and poor lifestyle choices. It is probable that you may be engaging in excessive or inadequate sleep patterns. One might consume excessive alcohol, indulge excessively in food, or abstain from eating altogether. These are all valid, substantiated rationales for your diminished energy levels, which impede your ability to accomplish your daily tasks.

Improving Your Energy

How can you enhance your energy levels to ensure sufficient stamina for all the tasks listed on your agenda? Please adhere to the following recommendations:+

Ensure that you obtain a minimum of 8 hours of sleep on a daily basis. This period is dedicated to your recuperation and cannot be casually forfeited or substituted without adequate justification. Should you be aware of a demanding schedule ahead, we recommend allocating your leisure time for self-revitalization rather than engaging in television consumption. If you are allocating a portion of your rest period for work or pressing matters, the trade-off should be deemed justifiable.

Consume food appropriately, meaning in the optimal quantity, at the appropriate timings, and with careful selection of suitable dietary options. It is imperative to recognize that breakfast holds significant importance as the foremost meal of the day. It is essential for your meal to primarily consist of vegetables, accompanied by a suitable source of protein. Additionally, it is recommended to consume a minimum of 8 glasses of water daily.

Engage in physical stretching and exercise, particularly during the morning hours. It would be advisable to incorporate this into your daily Rhythm Routine or Recipe to facilitate its habit formation. The prevailing belief amongst the majority is that physical exercise predominantly serves the purpose of weight reduction. However, this notion is, in fact, mistaken. Physical activity contributes to the elevation of heart rate, thereby facilitating the circulation of warmed blood throughout the entire body. Upon engaging in this activity, it shall come to your attention that all of your bodily organs and appendages are roused, inducing a state of increased vigor and enthusiasm for the forthcoming day. You may find it astonishing how significantly more efficacious this is in comparison to coffee.

Options For Work-Life Balance

The heading of this chapter conveys significant insights into the genuine essence of managing time. Should you currently hold the belief that each strategy enumerated in the preceding chapter will prove effective in your situation, I regret to inform you that you are mistaken. My apologies for any lack of clarity in earlier communication; unexpected circumstances do add excitement to life, after all.

Ultimately, the responsibility for managing one's time lies in one's hands, taking into account the lifestyle one leads. Select the methodologies that are most effective for your circumstances.

One of the primary rationales behind the concept of time management stems from the imperative of attaining a harmonious equilibrium between one's professional and personal spheres. The objective of this chapter is to present a range of choices that you can selectively choose from based on the specific circumstances of your life. For example, a method that is highly likely to be applicable for entrepreneurs, who frequently operate within unpredictable time frameworks, may not be as feasible for office employees, who adhere to specific schedule and routines.

The crux of the matter lies in attaining optimal productivity through the implementation of whichever strategy you deem fit, thereby attaining the well-deserved equilibrium between work and personal life. Taking this into consideration, presented below are some recommendations on how to achieve a harmonious and gratifying equilibrium between professional commitments and personal obligations.

Simplify your work.

A potential approach to attain a harmonious work-life balance is to streamline and reduce the complexity of your professional responsibilities. This technique aligns significantly with the recommendations provided in the preceding chapter, including the deliberate selection of Most Important Tasks, effective delegation, and streamlining of assignments.

To streamline your tasks entails approaching them methodically and terminating progress as necessary. Simplifying workload can be encapsulated by this counsel: Avoid being excessively diligent in your professional pursuits.

An individual consumed by work takes on excessive responsibilities, operating under the belief that increased workload correlates with heightened productivity, leading to greater achievements and increased fulfillment. If you adopt this approach towards work, allow me to present a contemplation: Does the act of exerting additional effort truly result in heightened personal fulfillment? Does work represent the sole avenue through which one can attain a feeling of accomplishment?

The core principle of maintaining work-life balance lies in acknowledging that work constitutes merely a component of one's life, which is encompassed by other facets of equivalent or greater significance, such as the familial realm.

Establish a clear distinction between one's professional and personal spheres.

Streamlining your workload is undoubtedly a more challenging endeavor, particularly if you happen to be an entrepreneur or business proprietor, or alternatively, if you are an employee juggling multiple projects concurrently. If the feasibility of simplifying and reducing workload appears remote, adopting a strategic approach in distinguishing your professional and personal domains can be an effective measure to integrate into your daily routine.

For businessmen and women, a highly effective method involves disengaging from technology, thereby entailing the act of powering down personal phones and devices or activating airplane mode when within one's residence. Do you have any high-priority matters that necessitate your attention and the need to receive frequent work-related phone calls and messages? If you are an entrepreneur overseeing business operations and find yourself invariably indispensable, perhaps it is opportune to consign and entrust significant responsibilities to competent members within your team. Furthermore, technology can prove to be immensely advantageous in effectively managing your business or project. Proceed with the installation of the designated software, establish a proficient operating system, or make use of the voice mail feature. There exist methods to maintain accessibility without the necessity of immediately responding to each incoming call, email, or message as soon as it arises. Ensure transparency regarding your periods of unavailability and communicate this information to all relevant parties, including clients, to provide them with a definitive timeframe during which they may reach out to you.

For office-based employees, establishing a clear boundary between work and personal life can be easily achieved by adhering to a strict schedule, such as leaving work premises by 5pm or at the conclusion of one's designated shift. Please refrain from developing a precedent of working additional hours. Naturally, there may arise circumstances in which it becomes necessary for you to extend your working hours in order to complete a task or provide assistance. However, it is imperative that such occurrences do not become habitual. Maintain self-respect and value your time.

Please keep in mind that it is imperative to maintain a healthy work-life equilibrium, irrespective of the field or nature of your occupation.

Harmonize work and personal commitments.

As previously stated, the purpose of time management is to facilitate the attainment and sustainability of a harmonious equilibrium between one's work and personal life. There exist certain lifestyles that render the achievement of this equilibrium seemingly unattainable or arduous. An instance of this phenomenon can be observed in the lifestyle of an entrepreneur, who frequently necessitates continuous engagement and commitment round the clock. Those individuals who adhere to such a lifestyle may perceive equilibrium as an unattainable aspiration.

Achieving a harmonious equilibrium between work and personal life does not necessarily have to pose as a formidable challenge. If establishing a clear delineation between your personal and professional domains proves to be challenging, consider instead striving to harmonize and integrate these facets of your life.

An effective approach would be to enlist the participation of your family and friends. For example, rather than engaging an unfamiliar individual to participate in one of your business endeavors, it might be prudent to contemplate the involvement of a family member, friend, or relative who possesses relevant expertise. By adopting this approach, you are effectively accomplishing two objectives simultaneously: enhancing the bond between you and also completing the necessary tasks.

One can also integrate their personal and professional spheres by cultivating relationships with their colleagues and professional acquaintances. Some individuals may vehemently refrain from combining their social relationships with their professional endeavors, however, is there not room for flexibility and exploration in this regard? One can establish companionship with individuals from all walks of life.

If one is contemplating the establishment of a business and harbors the desire to synchronize their entrepreneurial pursuits with their personal life, it would be advantageous to engage one's partner or spouse in the endeavor. Numerous prosperous and accomplished enterprises, which endure and thrive for extended periods, are those operated by family units. Incorporating your family into the operations of your business facilitates the attainment of optimal performance at work, all the while allowing for quality time to be spent with your family members or relatives. Rather than exerting excessive effort in delineating a distinct boundary between one's professional and personal spheres, why not integrate them seamlessly?

This serves as a potential solution for you to contemplate if you are seeking to effectively manage your time and attain equilibrium.

Segregate roles.

Efficiently managing one's time can prove to be a significant challenge for individuals who find themselves juggling multiple roles and responsibilities. For individuals employed in various capacities, including laborers and all other individuals adhering to strictly defined work schedules, it is comparatively effortless to establish demarcations and unambiguously designate specific timeframes within each day and week for personal or domestic activities. For individuals operating as entrepreneurs, artists, caretakers, or those devoid of a fixed timetable, striking a harmonious equilibrium between professional and personal lives can prove to be an arduous task which demands relinquishing certain facets of their vocational occupation.

One possible approach to address this concern is to perceive "time" as merely comprising half of a complete entity. The remaining fifty percent is allocated for the purpose of carrying out various "responsibilities." Certain individuals have assigned responsibilities within a designated timeframe. An apt illustration of this can be seen through the case of an employee. Specifically, Jenny, on every weekday at 8 am, commutes to her workplace, temporarily setting aside her responsibilities as a wife and mother. By 9 am, Jenny assumes the role of a department head within a prominent corporation, exhibiting deep dedication to her work and consistently garnering exceptional outcomes for the organization. At 5pm, Jenny concludes her work day fatigued yet content, and returns to her family residence. Subsequently, she reengages in her duties as a mother and wife, in addition to her other responsibilities. During the course of Saturdays, she assumes various roles such as yogi Jenny, companion and shopping confidant Jenny, and blogger Jenny. On Sundays, she assumes the identity of Jenny the churchgoer, Jenny the daughter, and so forth. In general, Jenny effortlessly discerns her designated role on particular weekdays, as well as during specified hours each day on the set.

As evidenced by the given example, Jenny assumes various responsibilities throughout the course of both her daily and weekly routines. The inherent nature of her work readily allows for the identification of the specific roles she will be undertaking. For individuals who find their professional and personal domains intersecting during their daily routines, adopting a roles-based approach can be a viable strategy in achieving a harmonious work-life balance, as opposed to a strictly time-based approach.

Although the absence of fixed schedules may appear daunting, it can be leveraged to one's benefit. Please outline all the roles you fulfill and responsibilities you assume, and subsequently indicate the optimal timing for performing each of these roles throughout the day. As a parent who dedicates themselves to their children's upbringing and a writer, it is important to establish a clear distinction between your responsibilities as a mother or father and your obligations as a writer. As an illustration, after you have seen to the task of taking your children to school and accomplishing errands, allow yourself some additional time for a smooth transition into your subsequent responsibility, such as the role of a writer. Utilize this period to diligently engage in the act of writing. Ensure that you possess a thorough understanding of your most optimal writing period, during which you experience heightened energy levels or creativity, and encounter minimal interruptions or preoccupations. This scheme is designed to accommodate your needs, rather than expecting you to conform to its demands.

Engage in the exploration of this technique and carefully observe the periods within each day and days within the week wherein you reach your optimal state and exhibit the highest levels of productivity. This will facilitate the monitoring of your progress and enable you to attain the desired equilibrium.

Please make efficient use of your allotted work hours.

Frequently, individuals lament their dearth of personal time while squandering valuable hours in their professional endeavors. In order to fully embrace your personal and domestic life, it is essential to optimize your productivity in the workplace and refrain from engaging in non-essential activities.

Prior to effectively managing your time, it is imperative to ensure that the tasks you undertake consistently contribute to the ultimate outcome of your desired objectives. Do not become excessively preoccupied with trivial matters, such as fixating on absolute flawlessness, deferring action until finding the ideal catalyst for motivation, and excessively prioritizing quantity over the caliber of work. Becoming excessively engrossed in these work-related factors often deprives individuals of their time, leading to additional hours, or potentially developing workaholic tendencies. Please bear in mind that it is more effective to employ efficient strategies rather than exerting excessive effort. Acquire the knowledge of efficiently utilizing each minute and hour to benefit yourself, thereby ensuring that you also allocate time for your personal life, a paramount aspect of existence which should never be compromised.

www.ingramcontent.com/pod-product-compliance
Lightning Source LLC
Chambersburg PA
CBHW050232120526
44590CB00016B/2059